T0273773

BEFORE USING...

 Before using this book, please read the guidelines inside the back cover. For a free copy of the detailed guidelines go to www.hunterhouse.com or call the ordering number below.

 To prevent bleed-through, it is recommended that water-based, rather than spirit-based, markers or pens be used in this Workbook.

MY OWN THOUGHTS AND FEELINGS (FOR BOYS)

A Hunter House Growth and Recovery Workbook
by Wendy Deaton, M.A., M.F.C.C.
Series consultant: Kendall Johnson, Ph.D.

ISBN-10: 1-63026-824-0   ISBN-13: 978-1-63026-824-4

ORDERING INFORMATION

Additional copies of this and other Growth and Recovery Workbooks may be obtained from Hunter House. Bulk discounts are available for professional offices and recognized organizations.

All single workbooks: $11.95

THE GROWTH AND RECOVERY WORKBOOKS (GROW) SERIES

A creative, child-friendly program designed for use with elementary-school children, filled with original exercises to foster healing, self-understanding, and optimal growth.

Workbooks for children ages 9–12 include:

No More Hurt—provides a safe place for children who have been physically or sexually abused to explore and share their feelings

Living with My Family—helps children traumatized by domestic violence and family fights to identify and express their fears

Someone I Love Died—for children who have lost a loved one and who are dealing with grief, loss, and helplessness

A Separation in My Family—for children whose parents are separating or have already separated or divorced

Drinking and Drugs in My Family—for children who have family members who engage in regular alcohol and substance abuse

I Am a Survivor—for children who have survived an accident or fire, or a natural disaster such as a flood, hurricane, or earthquake

I Saw It Happen—for children who have witnessed a traumatic event such as a shooting at school, a frightening accident, or other violence

Workbooks for children ages 6–10 include:

My Own Thoughts and Feelings (for Girls); My Own Thoughts and Feelings (for Boys)—for exploring suspected trauma and early symptoms of depression, low self-esteem, family conflict, maladjustment, and nonspecific dysfunction

My Own Thoughts on Stopping the Hurt—for exploring suspected trauma and communicating with young children who may have suffered physical or sexual abuse

We welcome suggestions for new and needed workbooks

DISCLAIMER

This book is intended as a treatment tool for use in a therapeutic setting. It is not intended to be utilized for diagnostic or investigative purposes. It is not designed for and should not be recommended or suggested for use in any unsupervised or self-help or self-therapy setting, group, or situation whatsoever. Any professionals who use this book are exercising their own professional judgment and take full responsibility for doing so.

You are SPECIAL.
Write or draw your name
in a way that shows
how you are special.

Begin a list of special things you like about yourself.

_____

_____

_____

_____

_____

_____

_____

_____

_____

_____

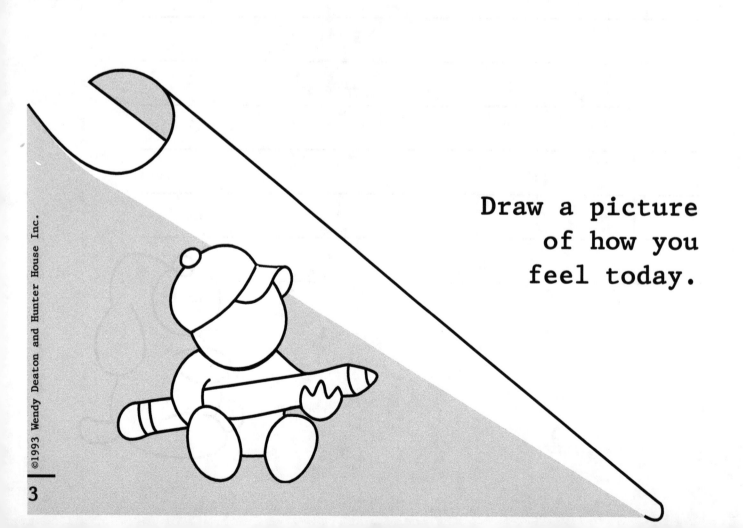

Draw a picture
of how you
feel today.

What is your favorite animal? Draw a picture of your animal and write three things you like about this animal.

1. _____

2. _____

3. _____

Make a list of things you can do yourself.

Everyone has feelings.
Here are some:

angry

sad

lonesome

guilty

scared

excited   loving

giggly   upset

embarrassed

worried

silly

unhappy

happy

mad

Circle the feelings
you have had.

Write any other feelings you have:

_____

_____

Complete the following lines:

Something that scares me is

_____

_____

Something that makes me happy is

_____

_____

I feel mad when

_____

_____

I feel sad when

_____

_____

I feel bad when

_____

_____

I feel good when

_____

_____

Answer YES if you ever had
these worries, and NO if you
never had this worry.

Do you worry about what is happening in your family? _____

Do you worry about what is happening at school? _____

Do you worry about your friends? _____

Do you worry about bad grades at school? _____

Do you worry about not doing well at sports? _____

Do you worry that no one likes you? _____

Do you worry that your mom or dad has a problem? _____

Do you worry about earthquakes? _____

Do you worry about fires? _____

Do you worry about being alone? _____

Do you worry about a war? _____

Do you worry about being sick? _____

Do you have other worries? List your other worries? _____

_____

Write all your worries
on this trashbag and
forget them for now!

Do you agree ✓ or disagree ✗

- [ ] I am a good person.
- [ ] The world is a good place.
- [ ] It's okay to say what you feel.
- [ ] Sometimes parents fight and it's okay.
- [ ] It's okay to cry.
- [ ] Parents should live together.
- [ ] Sometimes people in a family don't like each other and it's okay.
- [ ] Everyone has a right to private things.
- [ ] Everyone has a right to his or her own feelings.
- [ ] It's okay to be sad.
- [ ] It's okay to be mad.
- [ ] Kids have a right to say No to adults.
- [ ] Feelings are okay.
- [ ] Growing up can be a good thing.
- [ ] You can help yourself to be happier.
- [ ] I deserve to be loved.

©1993 Wendy Deaton and Hunter House Inc.

1. Have your counselor tell a story, and you can draw the pictures on the next two pages.

OR

2. Write a story and draw the pictures using one of these titles:

- The Little Prince or The Little Princess

- The Nightmare

- Mom's House and Dad's House

- When Wishes Come True

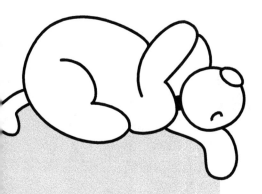

Everyone makes
mistakes. Tell about
a BIG mistake
you made.

Write about the HAPPIEST
thing that ever happened
to you.

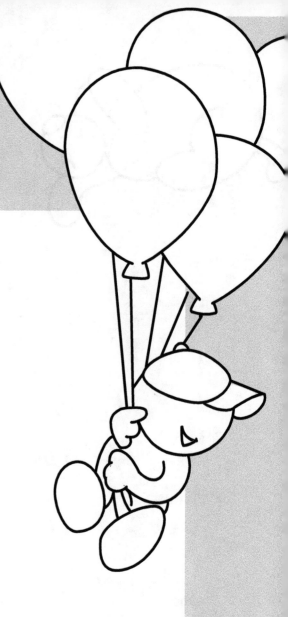

Write or
draw a picture
about something that
changed your life forever.

Sometimes you may wish you could change some things in your life. You might want to change where you live, your school, or how tall you are.

Make a list of things you can change by yourself.

_____

_____

_____

Make a list of things you could change if you had help.

_____

_____

_____

Make a list of things you wish you could change, that you can't change even though you want to.

_____

_____

_____

Everyone has angry feelings at times. Sometimes when you have angry feelings you feel like hurting yourself or someone else, or like breaking something.
Write about a time when you were angry. What did you do?

©1993 Wendy Deaton and Hunter House Inc.

Make a list of things you can do when you are angry that are good things to do and that will help you feel better.

_____

_____

_____

_____

_____

_____

_____

_____

_____

Everyone sometimes feels
scared, sad, and hurt.
Even grown-up men and boys
feel these feelings.
Write or draw a picture
about a time when you felt
one of these feelings.

Here are some things you can do when you are scared, sad, or hurt:

- ask someone to stay with you
- ask for information about what bothers you
- turn on the lights in the dark
- lock the door
- play the radio
- tell someone in your family how you feel
- tell a friend how you feel
- cry
- get a hug
- play a fun game
- make hot chocolate

List some other things you can do that will make you feel better.

_____

_____

_____

Complete the following lines:

If I need help with homework I can ask _____.

If I need a hug I can ask _____.

If I need someone to talk to I can ask _____.

When I feel lonely, I can ask _____.

If I need help with angry feelings I can ask _____.

If I need help with sports I can ask _____.

If I need someone to play with I can ask _____.

If I need someone to help with feelings I can ask _____.

©1993 Wendy Deaton and Hunter House Inc.

Write a letter to someone special and tell them something you have not been able to talk to them about in person.

Dear _____,

☐ Love lasts forever.

☐ Love sometimes hurts.

☐ Love is scary.

☐ Love means I'll love only you.

☐ Love means never being jealous.

☐ Feelings of love can change.

☐ Love means never being lonely.

☐ Love means never being selfish.

☐ There are lots of kinds of love.

☐ The more people you love, the more love you have.

☐ Love means giving to others.

☐ Love means getting from others.

☐ Love keeps growing.

Draw a picture of you
doing your favorite
activity.

A hero or heroine is someone you look up to because they are brave, smart, strong, or have done something important.
When we try to be like a hero or heroine we can sometimes do our very best.

Name three people you
think of as heroes or heroines.

1. _____

2. _____

3. _____

Write what you like about your heroes
and heroines.
Or draw a picture of you and one of your
heroes or heroines.

If you were going to be in a race, what kind of race would it be?

- [ ] running
- [ ] bicycles
- [ ] cars
- [ ] boats
- [ ] skis
- [ ] skateboards
- [ ] horses

What others?

_____

_____

_____

If you were in a game or sport, what would it be?

- [ ] soccer
- [ ] baseball
- [ ] volleyball
- [ ] football
- [ ] tennis
- [ ] softball
- [ ] basketball

What others? _____

_____

What are all the things you need to win?

- [ ] patience
- [ ] speed
- [ ] strong arms
- [ ] power
- [ ] bravery
- [ ] luck
- [ ] desire to win
- [ ] quick turns
- [ ] strength
- [ ] practice
- [ ] strong legs
- [ ] brains
- [ ] courage

What else? _____

_____

These are the same things you can use to help you feel strong and safe now.

Make a list of three things you would like to be when you grow up.

1. _____

   _____

2. _____

   _____

3. _____

   _____

Tell what you would like about each of these things.

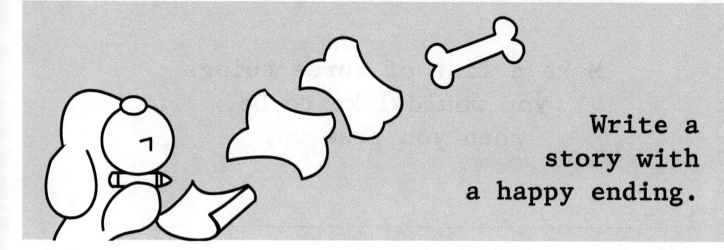

Write a
story with
a happy ending.

Make three wishes
for yourself and your family.

PLEASE READ THIS...

This is a brief guide to the design and use of the Growth and Recovery (GROW) workbooks from Hunter House. It is excerpted from detailed guidelines that can be downloaded from www .hunterhouse.com or are available free through the mail by calling the ordering number at the bottom of the page. Please consult the detailed guidelines before using this workbook for the first time.

GROW workbooks provide a way to open up communication with children who are not able to or who are reluctant to talk about a traumatic experience. They are not self-help books and are not designed for guardians or parents to use on their own with children. They address sensitive issues, and a child's recovery and healing require the safety, structured approach, and insight provided by a trained professional.

Each therapist will bring her own originality, creativity, and experience to the interaction and may adapt the tasks and activities in the workbooks, using other materials and activities. With less verbally oriented children, the use of art therapy or music or video may be recommended, or certain exercises may be conducted in groups.

Each pair of facing pages in the workbook provides the focus for a therapeutic "movement" that may take up one session. However, more than one movement can be made in a single session or several sessions may be devoted to a single movement. Children should be allowed to move through the process at their own pace. If a child finds a task too "hot" to approach, the therapist can return to it later. When something is fruitful it can be pursued with extended tasks.

While a therapist is free to select the order of activities for each child, the exercises are laid out in a progression based on the principles of critical incident stress management:

- initial exercises focus on building the therapeutic alliance
- the child is then led to relate an overview of the experience
- this is deepened by a "sensory-unpacking" designed to access and recover traumatic memories
- family experiences and changed living conditions, if any, are explored
- emotions are encouraged, explored, and validated.
- delayed reactions are dealt with, and resources are explored.
- the experience is integrated into the child's life through a series of strength-building exercises.

Specific pages in the GROW workbooks are cross-referenced to Dr. Kendall Johnson's book *Trauma in the Lives of Children* (Hunter House, Alameda, 1998). This provides additional information on the treatment of traumatized children.

The content of the workbooks should be shared with parents or significant adults only when the child feels ready for it and if it is therapeutically wise. Workbooks should not be given to children to take home until the therapeutic process is completed according to the therapist's satisfaction.

Although this series of workbooks was written for school-age children, the tasks are adaptable for use with younger children and adolescents.

Detailed guidelines are available for each GROW workbook (see list on front inside cover).